Little Red Ladybug

by Liza Charlesworth
illustrated by Jim Paillot

SCHOLASTIC

New York ✳ Toronto ✳ London ✳ Auckland
Sydney ✳ Mexico City ✳ New Delhi ✳ Hong Kong

To my
excellent cousin
Emmett

ISBN 978-0-545-68630-3

12 11 10 9 8 7 6 5 4 3 2 1   14 15 16 17 18 19/0

Printed in China.

Once upon a time, there lived a bug who
always wore a shiny red polka-dotted coat.
Everyone called her Little Red Ladybug.

One day, Little Red Ladybug's mother said, "Your grandma is sick. Go into the forest and pick some flowers. Then take them to Granny Bug to cheer her up."

Little Red Ladybug's mother kissed her
good-bye. "Stay on the path," she said.
"That way, you won't get into any trouble."
"I will," promised Little Red Ladybug.

Little Red Ladybug crept along the forest
path. By and by, she saw a patch of sunny,
yellow flowers. She put some in her basket.

Next Little Red Ladybug saw a patch of sky blue flowers. She put some in her basket.

Next Little Red Ladybug saw a patch of ruby red flowers. My, they were lovely! She put down her basket to pick some.

Lickety-split, a huge wolf spider jumped onto the path.

"Howl do you do?" said the Big Bad Wolf Spider. "I don't mean to bug you, but where are you going?"

"I'm going to Granny Bug's house," replied Little Red Ladybug. "She's sick, so I'm picking some flowers to cheer her up."

"How delightful! There are some pretty pink flowers right over there," said the wolf spider. He pointed deep into the woods.

"I promised my mother I'd stay on the path," Little Red Ladybug said. "But pink *is* my grandma's favorite color."

So off she crept to pick the flowers.

"Good-bye," said the wolf spider with a wave.

Then away he scurried to Granny Bug's house.

Knock, knock, knock.

"Who's there?" asked Granny Bug sweetly.

"It's Little Red Ladybug," lied the wolf spider.

"Oh, I'll let you right in," she replied.

When Granny Bug opened the door, the Big Bad Wolf Spider grabbed her. Lickety-split, he used his spider silk to tie her to a chair.

"You'll be perfect for my dinner," he said.

"Now I just have to wait for my dessert to arrive."

By and by, Little Red Ladybug got to Granny
Bug's house. *Knock, knock, knock.*

"Come in, dear!" said a voice.

Little Red Ladybug crept inside. Poor Granny
Bug didn't look well at all!

"What big eyes you have," said Little Red Ladybug, "and there are so many of them!"

"All the better to see you with," replied the wolf spider.

"What long, hairy arms you have," said
Little Red Ladybug, "and there are so many of
them!"

"All the better to hug you with," replied the
wolf spider.

"And what big fangs you have!" said Little
Red Ladybug.

"All the better to eat you with!" replied the
wolf spider.

Lickety-split, he used his spider silk to tie Little
Red Ladybug to a chair beside her grandma.

Then the Big Bad Wolf Spider went into the kitchen to cook a pot of fly soup to go with his meal.

But there was something he didn't know about pretty ladybugs. They have *very* powerful jaws. Little Red Ladybug and Granny Bug chewed and chewed and chewed until . . .

. . . they were both free!

When the Big Bad Wolf Spider came back—
guess what? Little Red Ladybug and her
grandma tied him up with his very own spider silk!

Then they called the pest police, who put the Big Bad Wolf Spider in a place where he could not bug anyone. And he spent the rest of his life making teeny socks for centipedes.

As for the ladybugs, they lived happily ever after. Granny Bug got better and Little Red Ladybug kept visiting with baskets of bright flowers. But she *never ever* crept off the forest path again.

Comprehension Boosters

1 Retell this story in your own words.

2 Why did the Big Bad Wolf Spider tell Little Red Ladybug about the pink flowers?

3 Can you think of five great words to describe Little Red Ladybug? How about the Big Bad Wolf Spider?

4 What important lesson did Little Red Ladybug learn?

5 What happens *after* the ladybugs live happily ever after? Turn on your imagination and tell a story about it!